EDGE BOOKS

TOP SECRET FILES

SECRETS OF WORLD WAR II

BY SEAN McCOLLUM

raintree

a Capstone company — publishers for children

Raintree is an imprint of Capstone Global Library Limited, a company incorporated in England and Wales having its registered office at 264 Banbury Road, Oxford, OX2 7DY – Registered company number: 6695582

www.raintree.co.uk
myorders@raintree.co.uk

Text © Capstone Global Library Limited 2017
The moral rights of the proprietor have been asserted.

All rights reserved. No part of this publication may be reproduced in any form or by any means (including photocopying or storing it in any medium by electronic means and whether or not transiently or incidentally to some other use of this publication) without the written permission of the copyright owner, except in accordance with the provisions of the Copyright, Designs and Patents Act 1988 or under the terms of a licence issued by the Copyright Licensing Agency, Saffron House, 6–10 Kirby Street, London EC1N 8TS (www.cla.co.uk). Applications for the copyright owner's written permission should be addressed to the publisher.

Edited by Nate LeBoutillier
Designed by Steve Mead
Picture research by Pam Mistakos
Production by Laura Manthe

ISBN 978 1 4747 3527 8 (hardback)
20 19 18 17 16
10 9 8 7 6 5 4 3 2 1

ISBN 978 1 4747 3529 2 (paperback)
21 20 19 18 17
10 9 8 7 6 5 4 3 2 1

British Library Cataloguing in Publication Data
A full catalogue record for this book is available from the British Library.

Acknowledgements
Bridgeman Images: Inflatable Light Tank used in England for Operation Fortitude, 1944 (Operation Overlord), 13, The Stapleton Collection, 23 bottom; Getty Images: The Stanley Weston Archive, 16, Universal History Archive, 23 top right; Granger: ullstein bild/Granger, NYC - All rights reserved, 17; Newscom: Everett Collection, 15, R Chandler News Syndication, 25; Shutterstock: Dmitrijs Mihejevs, 18, Everett Collection, cover, Everett Historical, 2-3, 4-5, 7, 9, 10-11, 14, 19, 26, 27, 28; Wikimedia: Executive Office of the President of the United States, 20, U.S. Navy, 21, Naval Historical Center, 24

Shuttertsock: Design Elements, Davor Ratkovic, javarman, STILLFX, yoshi0511

Every effort has been made to contact copyright holders of material reproduced in this book. Any omissions will be rectified in subsequent printings if notice is given to the publisher.

All the internet addresses (URLs) given in this book were valid at the time of going to press. However, due to the dynamic nature of the internet, some addresses may have changed, or sites may have changed or ceased to exist since publication. While the author and publisher regret any inconvenience this may cause readers, no responsibility for any such changes can be accepted by either the author or the publisher.

Printed and bound in India.

CONTENTS

THE ROAD TO TOTAL WAR

Germany was in ruins after its defeat in World War I (1914–1918). This helped give rise to the Nazi Party. The Nazis promised to make the country powerful again. In the 1930s, they seized control of the government with Adolf Hitler as their leader.

Germany secretly began rebuilding its military forces. Afraid of getting into another disastrous war, other countries were slow to confront the threat.

On the other side of the world, Imperial Japan was pursuing goals similar to Nazi Germany's. In the 1930s, Japanese troops invaded parts of China. In 1939, Germany launched its plan to conquer Europe. Country after country was drawn into the fighting.

Nazi Party members ↑

World War II was fought on a huge scale. It featured sneak attacks, secret codes and top-secret spy missions. It unleashed the deadliest secret weapon ever made. Military forces were not the only targets. It soon became clear that cities and **civilians** would not be spared.

It was total war.

civilian a person who is not in the military

CHAPTER ONE

SNEAK ATTACKS – FAST AND FURIOUS

World War II started with a series of surprise attacks. Both Nazi Germany and Imperial Japan hoped to surprise their enemies in order to get the upper hand.

"BLITZKRIEG"

On 1 September 1939, German forces invaded Poland, starting World War II. The German offensive teamed infantry with fast-moving armour. Stuka dive bombers struck from the sky. These attacks pierced the Poles' defences then destroyed them. British reporters called the strategy *blitzkrieg*, German for "lightning war". Germany crushed Polish resistance in less than a month. The rest of Europe watched with alarm. The German war machine seemed unstoppable.

OPERATION BARBAROSSA

In June 1941, Nazi Germany launched Operation Barbarossa against the Soviet Union. It was a shocking betrayal. The Nazis and Soviets had signed a deal in 1939 that they would not attack each other. In fact, the Soviet army joined the Germans to overrun Poland. By early 1941, though, the Germans controlled most of Western Europe. This freed German forces to turn on the Soviet Union with the largest invasion force in history.

ALLIED POWERS (MAIN COUNTRIES)	AXIS POWERS
Great Britain (and its colonies) Soviet Union United States France China	Germany Japan Italy

www.southdublinlibraries.ie

FIGHTING FACT Stuka planes had wailing sirens. The sound effect made their force even more terrifying.

↑ German Army engineers cross the Vistula River in Poland.

JAPAN ATTACKS PEARL HARBOR

Japan's **ultimate** goal was to control all of Southeast Asia. In 1941 it secretly set in motion a bold plan to drive British and US forces from its side of the Pacific Ocean.

On 26 November 1941, the main Japanese attack fleet secretly sailed from Japan. Its target was the US naval base at Pearl Harbor, Hawaii. The fleet featured six aircraft carriers. Before dawn on 7 December they were in range. More than 350 planes took off from the Japanese carriers. The Americans were taken by complete surprise when these aircraft swept down from the sky. Dropping torpedoes and bombs, they destroyed 188 US planes and sunk or damaged nearly 20 ships. The attack triggered US entry into the war.

SOUTHEAST ASIA FALLS

Japanese forces staged surprise attacks across Southeast Asia within days of striking Pearl Harbor. They invaded Hong Kong, a British colony. They seized US bases on Guam and Wake Island. Within three months they had captured the British stronghold of Singapore and the US-controlled Philippines. By early 1942, Japan had much of the region in its grip.

FIGHTING FACT Japan used five top-secret mini-subs as part of its attack on Pearl Harbor. Each carried two torpedoes. Some evidence suggests one succeeded in torpedoing a US battleship.

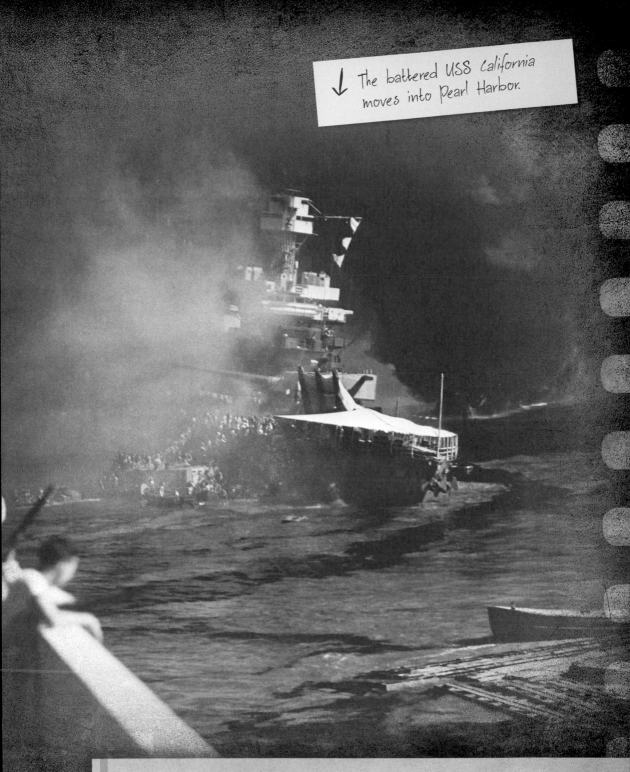

The battered USS California moves into Pearl Harbor.

ultimate greatest, most important

OPERATION URANUS

Soviet forces fell back as the German army pushed eastwards in 1941–42. However, the Soviets were able to spring a trap at the **besieged** city of Stalingrad. Called Operation Uranus, it stunned German commanders in November 1942. Soviet units pretended to be building defences, but instead attacked from the north. The next day a second group of Soviet forces sprang forward from the south. Soon the Soviets had encircled more than 250,000 enemy soldiers. The Soviet victory finally handed the Nazi war machine a major defeat.

German infantry moves into a burning Soviet village. ↓

THE BATTLE OF MIDWAY

In June 1942, Japanese and US fleets steamed towards a major battle near Midway Island. The Japanese force included four aircraft carriers, the Americans three. The ships sent wave after wave of torpedo bombers at the enemy. At one point US bombers hit the Japanese carriers while their decks were jammed with refuelling planes. This caused mass destruction. In the end, four Japanese carriers sank while the US lost one. The Japanese had hoped to lure the Americans into a trap and destroy its all-important aircraft carriers. The opposite happened. Now the US had the upper hand in the battle for the Pacific.

FIGHTING FACT

The United States had broken Japan's naval codes before the Battle of Midway. Therefore, US forces went into the fight knowing of Japanese plans to capture Midway Island.

besiege to surround with armed forces

SECRETS BEHIND THE FRONT LINES

One goal in warfare is to keep the enemy off-balance and confused. **Deception** played an important role throughout World War II.

THE DOOLITTLE RAID

After Pearl Harbor the United States was desperate for a chance to strike back. Japan, though, seemed out of reach. Then the US Navy proposed a daring, top-secret raid. On 18 April 1942, 16 B-25 bombers roared off the deck of an aircraft carrier 1,050 kilometres (650 miles) from Japan. Led by Colonel Jimmy Doolittle the pilots flew for Tokyo, Japan's capital. The aircraft dropped their bombs then crash-landed in China. The bombing did little damage but it shocked the Japanese. It also gave a big boost to American spirits.

FIGHTING FACT

In 1944 and 1945, Japan released more than 9,000 "balloon bombs". Air currents carried these bomb-carrying hydrogen balloons from Japan over North America. Only one exploded, killing a group of six people who found a crashed balloon in the state of Oregon.

Soldiers display an inflatable tank used in Operation Fortitude.

OPERATION FORTITUDE

In 1944, the Allies executed Operation Fortitude in locations throughout Europe. This plan created a phantom army of fake equipment to trick the Germans. It included inflatable tanks and planes built of wood. The Allies sent fake radio messages to support the hoax. The goal was to fool Axis spies about Allied strength and where the Allies planned to strike in Europe. The trickery helped the Allies succeed in landing a huge invasion force at Normandy, France, in June 1944.

deception something that makes people believe what is not true; a lie

ENIGMA AND ULTRA

German commanders used the Enigma machine to transmit their most important orders. It looked like a clunky keyboard, but Enigma scrambled messages in complex ways. Only another programmed Enigma machine could **decipher** them.

German leaders believed their codes were unbreakable. However, **cryptologists** from Poland, Britain and France gradually cracked them. This top-secret programme was code-named Ultra. Their efforts were aided when the British captured a German submarine in 1941. A working Enigma machine was found on board. As the war went on, the Allies knew more and more about German plans.

Enigma machine →

NAVAJO CODE TALKERS

Early in the war the US Marines recruited Navajo men. They created a code using their very complex Native American language. It had never been written down. Few non-Navajo had ever heard it. The Navajo Code Talkers allowed Marine units to transmit messages quickly. Standard secret messages had to be coded and decoded, taking precious time. Japanese codebreakers were baffled by words and sounds they had never heard. After an important battle, one US officer said, "Were it not for the Navajos, the Marines would never have taken Iwo Jima."

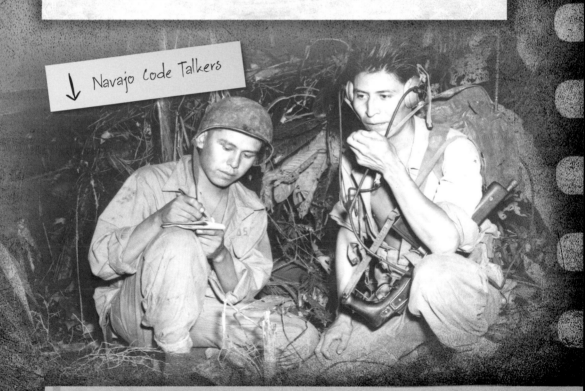

↓ Navajo Code Talkers

decipher to figure out something that is written in code or is hard to understand

cryptologist someone who studies codes

OPERATION GUNNERSIDE

Secret missions had the potential to change the course of the war – and history. In February 1943 a small team of Norwegian **commandoes** sneaked into a heavily guarded factory in German-**occupied** Norway. They rigged explosives then escaped. They skied 400 kilometres (250 miles) to safety while being hunted by German troops. The explosion destroyed the equipment German scientists were using to make a chemical known as "heavy water". This was an important ingredient for an atomic bomb. Operation *Gunnerside*, as it was called, helped block the Nazis from developing this super-weapon.

SPY CATCHER

Moe Berg played professional baseball in the US for 15 years. He was a decent player. He was also called "the brainiest guy in baseball". He spoke several languages and knew everything about world history and current events. Once the war started, he went to work as a spy for the US. He served undercover to keep tabs on Germany's efforts to build an atomic bomb.

OPERATION VALKYRIE

By 1944 the tide of war had turned against Germany. A group of German officers feared Hitler was leading the country to disaster. They plotted to take control of the government and make peace with the Allies. The first step was to kill Hitler in an operation called Valkyrie. On 20 July 1944, Colonel Claus von Stauffenberg sneaked a time bomb into a meeting, then left. The bomb blew the room to pieces and killed four people. Hitler, though, had been shielded by a heavy table. He suffered minor burns and a wounded arm. Operation Valkyrie had failed.

↓ Adolph Hitler's headquarters lay in ruins after failed Operation Valkyrie.

commando specially trained soldier used for secret missions

occupy to take possession or control by military invasion

THE FINAL SOLUTION

After Hitler took power in 1933, a nightmare unfolded in Europe. The Nazis imprisoned and killed people they considered "undesirable". Jews were at the top of the list. The Nazis blamed them for all of Germany's troubles.

"The Final Solution" was the Nazis' secret plan to wipe out Europe's Jews. Special units rounded up Jewish men, women and children. Some were executed on the spot. Some were forced to work in slave-labour camps. The Nazis also built extermination camps where prisoners were murdered with poison gas. This horrific episode in human history is remembered as the Holocaust.

↑ Auschwitz extermination camp

Prisoners stand in line at a concentration camp in Buchenwald.

FIGHTING FACT

About six million Jews were killed during the Holocaust – 1.5 million of them were children.

RESCUE OF THE DANISH JEWS

Nazi Germany invaded Denmark in April 1940. Three years later, the Nazis ordered all of the country's 7,800 Jews to be **deported** to concentration camps. The Danish resistance movement sprang into action. Danes helped hide their Jewish friends and neighbours. They were then smuggled in boats to Sweden, a **neutral** country. The rescue effort saved most of Denmark's Jews from certain death.

deport to forcefully send someone out of the country

neutral not supporting or agreeing with either side of a disagreement or competition

Holocaust the killing of millions of Jews and other people by the Nazis during World War II

CHAPTER THREE

NEW WEAPONS FOR A NEW KIND OF WAR

World War II introduced tactics and classes of weapons that revolutionized warfare.

SINKING THE *BISMARCK*

Before World War II, battleships were the kings of sea power. But a new kind of ship, the aircraft carrier with its planes, forever changed naval warfare. In May 1941, a powerful, new German battleship called *Bismarck* steamed into the Atlantic Ocean. It soon destroyed the British battlecruiser HMS *Hood*. Before *Bismarck* could escape, torpedo bombers from a British aircraft carrier caught up with it. A single torpedo wrecked *Bismark's* rudder so it could not steer. British ships then closed in for the kill.

FIGHTING FACT

In 1944 the USS *Finback*, a *Gato*-class submarine, rescued downed torpedo-bomber pilot George H.W. Bush. Forty-four years later Bush was elected president of the United States.

← USS *Finback*

GATO-CLASS SUBMARINES

In 1941, the US introduced *Gato*-class submarines. Seventy-seven were built, and most served in the Pacific. These subs were big, tough and stealthy. They could escape the enemy by diving as deep as 90 metres (300 feet). Their crews of 60–80 sailors could stay on patrol for 75 days at a time. This new class of submarine hurt the Japanese navy by sinking many military and supply ships.

RADAR AND THE BATTLE OF BRITAIN

By mid-1940, only Great Britain still stood against Nazi Germany in Western Europe. The *Luftwaffe*, Germany's air force, sent wave after wave of bombers and fighter planes to blast British cities.

British RAF pilots were outnumbered and outgunned, but they had a secret technology called Chain Home. Chain Home was a line of radar stations. It used radio waves to spot incoming aircraft. This early warning system gave RAF commanders 20 minutes warning about where *Luftwaffe* squadrons were headed. They could then send fighters where they were most needed. Chain Home helped block German plans to invade.

FLYING BOMBS AND FIGHTER JETS

After early victories, German forces were in full retreat by June 1944. Still, German engineers were firing up new weapons. One was the V-1 flying bomb. Powered by a newfangled jet engine, it could strike targets more than 240 kilometres (150 miles) away. Then came the V-2 rocket, the world's first long-range guided missile. In 1944 the *Luftwaffe* also flew the first fighter jet into battle, the Messerschmitt 262. But these advances came too late to prevent Nazi Germany's defeat.

FIGHTING FACT

RADAR stands for "Radio Detection and Ranging".

THE NAZI ROCKET SCIENTIST

Wernher von Braun was a member of the Nazi Party. He was also a genius of rocket science who oversaw the building of Germany's V-2 missile. He surrendered to the Americans immediately after the war. He and other German engineers were then transferred to the US. He later became the chief designer of the *Saturn V* rocket that launched US astronauts to the moon.

↓ A V-1 bomb lands in a street off Drury Lane in London.

BOOTS FROM THE SKY

Most land battles depended on "grunts" – **infantry** troops. Both sides experimented with strapping troops in parachutes and dropping them behind enemy lines. Often, though, these paratroopers landed far from their intended targets.

Still, paratroopers played an important role during Operation Overlord. This was the Allied invasion in June 1944 to retake France. Dropped the night of 6 June, paratroopers caused chaos behind German lines. They destroyed bridges and blocked roads to slow German **reinforcements**. This helped more than 150,000 Allied infantry come ashore near Normandy, France.

✓ Normandy Invasion

infantry a group of soldiers trained to fight and travel on foot

reinforcements extra troops sent to strengthen a fighting force

LANDMINES AND "BOUNCING BETTIES"

World War II saw widespread use of landmines. These were buried bombs that exploded when soldiers stepped on them. Anti-tank mines were also used to wreck advancing armour. The German S-mine proved very effective at slowing Allied infantry advances. Nicknamed "Bouncing Betty", it sprang into the air before exploding. One US officer described the S-mine as "probably the most feared device encountered by Allied troops in the war".

FIGHTING FACT

New technology introduced at Normandy on D-Day included a "swimming" tank, a flame-throwing tank called "the crocodile" and collapsible motorbikes.

THE RACE FOR THE ATOMIC BOMB

In the 1930s scientists realized **atomic** weapons could release tremendous power. Leaders on all sides soon recognized that whatever country possessed such weapons would win the war.

The Manhattan Project was the most top-secret Allied programme of World War II. An international team of more than 130,000 people worked on it, mainly in the US. Most did not even know the project's purpose – to build the first atomic bomb. American leaders feared Germany or the Soviet Union might beat them to it. The first atomic bomb was tested in New Mexico on 16 July 1945. The shock wave shattered windows in Silver City – 193 kilometres (120 miles) away.

An aerial view of Tachikawa, Japan, shows ruin left by bombing raids.

LITTLE BOY AND FAT MAN

In early May 1945 the Germans surrendered, ending the war in Europe. The Japanese were in retreat but still continued to fight. On 6 August, a single US bomber flew over Hiroshima, Japan. Minutes later there was a blinding flash and unbelievable explosion. The atomic bomb nicknamed "Little Boy" flattened the city in an instant. An estimated 80,000 people or more were killed. Three days later, another US plane dropped the "Fat Man" atomic bomb on Nagasaki. It killed tens of thousands more. Japan surrendered a few days later.

post-war model of an atomic bomb →

FIGHTING FACT
Spies for the Soviet Union stole important information from the Manhattan Project. The Soviets tested their own atomic bomb in 1949.

atomic relating to or concerned with atoms, atomic bombs or nuclear energy

THE DEADLIEST WAR

World War II was the deadliest, most destructive war in history — before or since. In earlier conflicts, military forces mainly targeted each other. The "total war" strategies of World War II broke all those rules.

Historians calculate anywhere from 50 to 85 million people died during World War II. They estimate civilians may have made up two-thirds of the dead. In the case of the Holocaust, innocent people were murdered just because of who they were. Bombing raids burned entire cities to the ground in Germany and Japan.

Secrets of all kinds were part of the fighting of World War II. Some secrets and deceptions killed while others saved lives. Soon after the end of World War II, though, everyone saw the truth about the next world war. If fought with atomic weapons, it could be the last war of all.

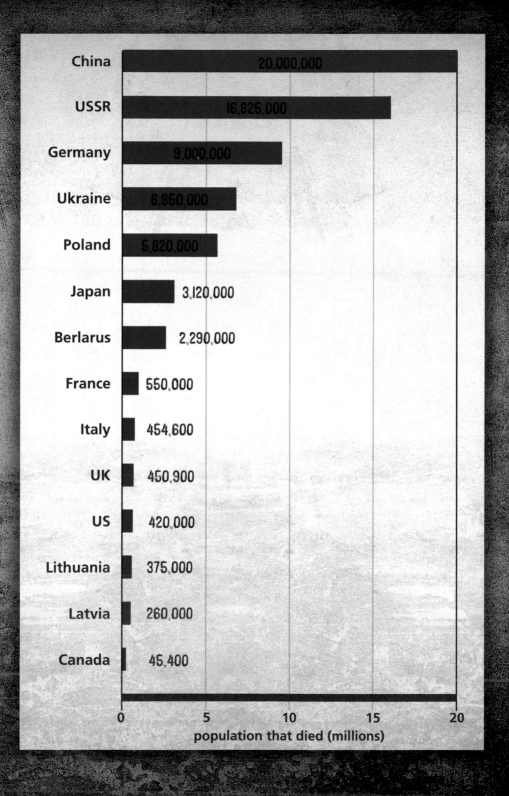

Country	population that died (millions)
China	20,000,000
USSR	16,825,000
Germany	9,000,000
Ukraine	6,850,000
Poland	5,820,000
Japan	3,120,000
Berlarus	2,290,000
France	550,000
Italy	454,600
UK	450,900
US	420,000
Lithuania	375,000
Latvia	260,000
Canada	45,400

population that died (millions)

GLOSSARY

atomic relating to or concerned with atoms, atomic bombs or nuclear energy

besiege to surround with armed forces

civilian a person who is not in the military

commando specially trained soldier used for secret missions

cryptologist someone who studies codes

deception something that makes people believe what is not true; a lie

decipher to figure out something that is written in code or is hard to understand

deport to forcefully send someone out of the country

Holocaust the killing of millions of Jews and other people by the Nazis during World War II

infantry a group of soldiers trained to fight and travel on foot

neutral not supporting or agreeing with either side of a disagreement or competition

occupy to take possession or control by military invasion

reinforcements extra troops sent to strengthen a fighting force

ultimate greatest, most important

COMPREHENSION QUESTIONS

1. Read the text on page 15. Why were the Navajo Code Talkers a valuable resource for the US military?

2. The Holocaust was a horrible event in human history. What happened during the Holocaust?

READ MORE

Air Raids in World War II (The History Detective Investigates), Martin Parsons (Wayland, 2015)

Heroes of World War II series (Raintree, 2016)

World War II (Mad, Bad and Just Plain Dangerous), John Townsend (Franklin Watts, 2013)

WEBSITES

www.bbc.co.uk/schools/primaryhistory/world_war2
Find out all about what life was like for adults and children in the UK during World War II.

www.ngkids.co.uk/history/world-war-two
Discover interesting World War II facts on the National Geographic website.

INDEX